Original title:
The Citrus Touch

Copyright © 2025 Creative Arts Management OÜ
All rights reserved.

Author: Dante Kingsley
ISBN HARDBACK: 978-1-80586-459-2
ISBN PAPERBACK: 978-1-80586-931-3

Sunlit Orchard

In the sun, they bounce and sway,
Lemons wearing shades all day.
Oranges giggle on the vine,
How they sparkle, oh so fine!

Limes are rolling down the hill,
Taking bets on which will spill.
Fruits in hats, what a sight,
Making juice in pure delight!

Nectar of Spring

Bees are buzzing here and there,
Tasting flavors, without care.
Grapefruits throw a garden dance,
While tangerines just take a chance!

In the grove, a party's planned,
Sours do the twist, so grand.
Sweet scent wafts from every nook,
A fruit parade, just take a look!

Zesty Reflections

In mirrors made of lemon peels,
Reflections show big, juicy meals.
Lemonades tickle funny bones,
As citrus sing their merry tones.

With every squirt, a giggle springs,
Citrus jokes beat all the kings.
Each fruit shares a punny tale,
Zestiness takes us down the trail!

Fruits of Elysium

Heaven's pantry stocked with glee,
Pineapples play the ukulele.
Mangoes dance in sheer delight,
As coconuts take silly flight!

Fruits in robes of festive hues,
Planning parties with their views.
Laughter fills the orchard air,
Zesty charms beyond compare!

Juicy Melodies

In the orchard, I slipped on a peel,
Fell with a squish, oh what a meal!
Oranges laughed as they rolled around,
Lemonade dreams keep popping out loud.

Grapefruits grinned, what a sight to see,
Peachy jokes from the cherry tree,
Limes are whistling a zesty tune,
Banana peels dance under the moon.

Citrus Reverberations

A tangerine tango, what a surprise,
With each little twist, the laughter flies,
Squeezed too tight, that orange did burst,
A citrus shower, now isn't that cursed?

Lemon drops bouncing like rubber balls,
While others roll down with the fruit stalls.
Chasing after, my legs in a knot,
The playful fruit has me tied in a plot.

Ripened Joy

The grapefruit gave me a playful wink,
'Beta carotene, you really do stink!'
Laughing so hard, I fell from my chair,
With zest in the air, I twisted my hair.

A lime joined in with a cheeky smile,
'You're looking quite sour, can we revile?'
We painted the town in shades of bright green,
In a fruit salad world, we reign supreme.

Citrus Haven

In a small citrus town where fun's a must,
Grapes grumble low while the citrics combust,
Mangoes giggle, they shed off their skin,
A ruckus erupts, let the fruit games begin!

Pineapples don sunglasses, looking real cool,
While watermelons wade in their splash pool,
Fun is the flavor in this fruity abode,
A joyful ride on the citrus road.

Citrus Kisses

When life gives you lemons, just pucker up,
Do a silly dance, drink from your cup.
Oranges giggle, grapefruits roar,
Let's squeeze some laughter, who could ask for more?

Limes roll by with a zestful cheer,
Tickling noses, bringing bright ideas.
With every slice, we discover glee,
In the fruit bowl's humor, we're all carefree!

Rind and Rapture

In a world where tangy dreams collide,
We laugh at the rind that we cannot hide.
Peeling back layers of citrus delight,
Making our laughter soar to new heights.

The zest of our lives sparkles and shines,
In every sweet joke, joy entwines.
With silly puns and fruity roles,
Our hearts burst open, embracing the jokes!

Lemon Light

Under the sun, lemons play hide and seek,
Witty little orbs, never shy or meek.
With a twist of their peels and a wink so bright,
They cheer the world with their zesty light.

A slice of humor in each citrus tale,
Lemonade wishes on a cheeky gale.
So let's sip and giggle with our friends so dear,
For every drop brings laughter and cheer!

Sunlit Citrus Dreams

In the orchard of humor, fruits take a chance,
Lemons do the tango while oranges prance.
With every bright squeeze, we break into play,
In sunlit dreams, we chase woes away!

Grapefruits blush as they take the stage,
With giggles and grins, we break every cage.
So gather 'round the juicy delight,
Creating laughter that feels just right!

Vibrant Zest

In the fridge, a lemon grins,
Hiding from the limes and sins.
It dreams of juicing grand affairs,
And tickles taste buds with its flares.

Oranges joke, they start a dance,
With fresh-cut peels, they take a chance.
They laugh and roll across the floor,
Creating tangy legends galore.

Orchard's Delight

Grapefruits gossip on the vine,
Planning pranks, oh what a time!
They giggle bright at morning dew,
In this zesty morning view.

Lemons play tag with those yawned soon,
While citrus birds sing a cartoon.
They squirt a sound, with every beat,
A symphony that can't be beat!

Zing of Midsummer

Pineapples start a beach parade,
In sunglasses, they're not afraid.
Coconuts roll, with a cheeky smile,
Making tourists stick around for a while.

Lime pies sit with a confident air,
Winking at folks who stopped to stare.
Each slice a burst of sunny cheer,
In this midsummer, full of beer!

Citrus Wonderlands

Squeezed a bit too tight, oh dear!
Lemonade fountains spread good cheer.
The laughs flow out, a fizzy spree,
As citrus critters dance with glee.

Kumquats swirl in a fruity mess,
With juicy gossip, nothing less.
They tumble down, a merry troupe,
In this wonderland of fruity scoop!

Tangy Murmurs

In a garden where lemons play,
Limes roll around in a zesty ballet,
Oranges giggle, they'll never stop,
As grapefruits bounce and do a hop.

With every splash of juice that squirts,
A jester in yellow with all its quirks,
Sour faces turn sweet in surprise,
When tarts become pies in disguise!

Squeezed out laughter fills the air,
A zany fruit race without a care,
Kiwis spark joy with each funny face,
While tangerines do a merry chase.

Mirthful slices on a plate,
Juggling fruits get carried away—wait!
They tumble down in citrus delight,
Making everyone giggle with pure delight!

Sweet Sunshine Serenade

In the morning, citrus bright,
Lemonade dreams take off in flight,
A wink from a lime, oh what a sight!
Sunshine giggles with pure delight.

Citrus band plays a jolly tune,
Dancing under the glowing moon,
Twirling and swirling, oh what a spree,
With every pluck, they sing with glee.

A sweet orange hops on the floor,
Tickling lemons, wanting more,
Grapefruits grinning, in good cheer,
Who knew fruits could bring such flair?

The melody lingers, fresh and bright,
Fruitful laughter fills the night,
Merry melodies echo far,
With every slice, we raise a jar!

Citrus Bliss

In a world where zest takes a bow,
Lemons laugh with furrowed brows,
To be sour is quite the jest,
When sweet oranges dance, they impress.

Grapefruits sparkle in lemon light,
Sours surprised to find it's all right,
Tangled in laughter, no time for gloom,
While lime trees giggle in full bloom.

A salad, a mix of quirks and funk,
Bananas cheer when the oranges dunk,
Berry jokes and citric puns,
In this fruit bowl, each better than tons!

Adventuring tastes lead to bliss,
Counting giggles, oh what a list,
Sucking on slices, sweet and bright,
Citrus joy is pure delight!

Sunset in an Orchard

As the sun dips low and paints the sky,
Oranges burst forth, oh my, oh my!
Lemons sway with a ticklish wind,
Buffoons of citrus go for a spin.

The sunset's hues, a zesty affair,
While limes craft tales without a care,
Grapefruits chuckle, casting long shadows,
As laughter erupts, like vibrant meadows.

In the orchard, stories dance and twirl,
Kumquats giggle as they swirl and whirl,
Satsumas laugh with each warm breeze,
While tangerines tease with playful ease.

In this twilight, fruits find their groove,
Each sunset brings a citrus move,
Joyful whispers as night takes flight,
In an orchard full of silly delight!

Tangy Dreams

In my dreams, I peel delight,
Lemons dance in the moonlight.
Limes wear hats, they look so fine,
Oranges juggle, oh what a time.

Grapefruits gossip, so they say,
Telling tales of the sun's ballet.
Mandarins twirl, a citrus waltz,
In the land where no one faults.

Here the pineapples sing in glee,
Bouncing around like they're so free.
Citrus zingers, bright and bold,
In this dreamland, worth their gold.

So I laugh, with slices round,
In this zesty world, joy is found.
Dancing fruit, in bright arrays,
Squeeze the fun in all our days.

Fragrant Reverie

In a garden of zesty cheer,
Citrus scents bring laughter near.
Lemons giggle, skittle about,
While tangerines let out a shout.

A grapefruit dressed in polka dots,
Cracks jokes like he's got the chops.
Swinging high on a lime green vine,
These fruity antics are simply divine.

I catch a whiff of orange zest,
Making noses crinkle in jest.
Scented breeze that tickles the nose,
In this fragrant land, anything goes.

So come indulge in citrus dreams,
Where laughter bursts like sunny beams.
With a dash of humor, let's all play,
In this fragrant reverie, hip-hip-hooray!

Squeeze of Sunshine

Juicy spritz in the morning light,
Squeeze a smile, it's pure delight.
Fruits assemble, ready for fun,
Making mischief under the sun.

Lemons roll like they own the day,
Grapes join in with a cheeky sway.
Limes chuckle, their puns so slick,
Slicing through giggles, oh so quick.

With a squirt of wit that's sweet,
Every zesty pun's a treat.
Tangerines are throwing their zest,
In this sunshine, we feel so blessed.

So grab a cup, let juicy laugh,
Sip the fun, oh what a half!
A squeeze of joy bursts forth in time,
Chasing clouds away, with fruity rhyme.

Golden Elixir

In a flask of citrus cheer,
Golden nectar brings us near.
Sipping joy in every drop,
Witty banter never stops.

Oranges winking, oh what fun,
Dancing with grapes under the sun.
With a splash, the laughter flows,
In this potion, humor grows.

Pineapples blend, swirling bright,
Crafting potions, pure delight.
Limes are bartenders, oh so spry,
Mixing laughs with every try.

So raise a glass to our elixir,
Sip the sunshine, let it mix ya.
With every cup, the giggles cheer,
In this golden treat, joy's always near.

Sunshine on the Tongue

In the garden, things get zesty,
A citrus fruit, it's feeling testy.
Lemons dancing with glee,
A playful flight of fancy spree.

Oranges giggle as they roll,
Tangerines whisper—oh, what a stroll!
Lime winks mischievously bright,
Messing with juicers all night.

Sweet and Sour Memories

When I was young, I had a fight,
With a grapefruit, it wasn't polite.
Lime threw shade with a twisty grin,
While the mango cheered for my win.

Pineapple laughed, "You're never sweet!"
Lemon pouted, "I can't take the heat!"
Memories squeeze, the taste is bold,
Citrus tales that never get old.

Citrus Breeze

A citrus breeze whispers my name,
Fruit flies giggle, it's quite the game.
Grapefruit skies in a tangy whirl,
Orange clouds, such a fruity twirl.

Lime waves hello, a green surprise,
Close your eyes and see the skies.
With every sip of sunny cheer,
Citrus mischief draws us near.

Lemonade Lull

In the heat, a jug so bright,
Lemonade dreams dance in the light.
Add some sugar, a sprinkle of fun,
Making magic in the sun.

A sip brings giggles, no doubt at all,
Cooling down with a citrus call.
When life gives lemons, don't you frown,
Just pour that joy all over town!

Citrus Rhapsody

Lemon drops fall from the sky,
Tickling my nose as they fly.
A lime just winked, such a tease,
It's joy in every breeze.

Grapefruit was doing a jig,
Dancing small, and oh so big.
Oranges laughed, a bright parade,
In the sun, their zest displayed.

I tried to catch a citrus kiss,
But ended up with citrus bliss.
Peeling joy with every bite,
Oh, the sweetness feels so right!

Lemonade dreams swirl around,
Where all the funny flavors found.
In this grove, we twist and twirl,
A fruity party, give it a whirl!

Citrus Within

Inside this orange, there's a joke,
Packed in tight, a citrus poke.
Squeeze it twice and you might find,
A wacky laugh and zest intertwined.

Lemon lives on the edge of cheer,
Always bright, never drear.
Limes are sly with a cheeky grin,
Waiting for trouble to begin.

Imagine tangerines in hats,
Twirling like a group of cats.
They spin and flip with such delight,
Making fun till the morning light.

Under the tree, the laughter rings,
As every fruit displays their flings.
With a wink, they dance and sing,
Sharing joy that they would bring!

Orange Slices of Time

Slices of time, oh so sweet,
Each one packed with a funny treat.
Nibbled here, a giggle there,
What a delight, nobody's bare!

Once an orange lost its peel,
Started rolling with great zeal.
Lemon said, 'You're out of line!'
But laughed as he sipped on lime.

Time hops on like a tangerine,
Bouncing here, like a scene unseen.
With every squeeze, a memory's made,
Fruitful fun that will never fade.

So let us laugh, embrace the zest,
Orange slices, simply the best.
Dancing in a sticky mess,
Life's a laugh, so just confess!

Lively Citrus Tales

In a grove where oranges play,
Lively tales brighten the day.
Lemons throw a party spree,
Inviting all their friends, you see.

Lime jokes float on lemon air,
Spread the giggles everywhere.
Grapefruit slips on a juicy pun,
Leaving us in endless fun!

Slice a lemon, watch it grin,
Squeeze the juice, let the fun begin.
Orange wild with a mischievous flair,
Makes us cackle without a care.

With citrus tales, we share the glee,
In this orchard, carefree and free.
Every fruit a giggling sprite,
Turning our day to pure delight!

Nectar in Bloom

In a grove where laughter grows,
Oranges wear their sunny clothes.
Lemons giggle, tart and bright,
As grapefruits join the silly fight.

Bees buzz by with jokes a-fuzz,
Pollinating all the buzz.
Grapes are rolling, feeling fine,
Claiming they're the best of wine!

Orchard's Heartbeat

In the orchard, a band of fruit,
Dancing in their summery suit.
Cherries pop to the beat,
While apples tango on their feet.

Bananas slip, with joy they'll fall,
Making juice of their missed call.
Limes chime in with a zesty cheer,
A concert only fruit can hear!

Zesty Reflections

Mirrors shine with citrus glow,
Lemons laugh, putting on a show.
Tangerines roll with glee,
Pondering how fun life can be.

In the sun, they take their stand,
A zesty crew, so simply planned.
With every squeeze, they feel alive,
In this wild fruit party, they thrive!

Citrus Cascade

Down the hill, a splash of juice,
Oranges racing, free to choose.
With every bounce, a playful grin,
They roll and tumble, let the fun begin!

Grapefruits shout, "Let's take a dive!"
A citrus pool, a sunny hive.
Splashes bright, under the sun,
This fruity party's just begun!

Flavorful Journeys

A lemon walked into a bar,
And asked for a glass of cheer.
The bartender winked and said,
"No limes allowed; they bring a sneer!"

Orange peels danced through the air,
Twisting with a lime's sly grin.
They laughed and rolled in zesty pairs,
Creating chaos in their din.

Tangerines plotted a fruit parade,
With grapefruits leading the way.
"No sour faces, let's masquerade!"
They shouted loud, ready to play.

A splash of juice, a silly splash,
Made everyone giggle and shake.
Citrus antics, a flavorful bash,
With laughter that no one could fake.

Fragrant Murmurs

Lemon and lime had a tiff,
Said one was too zesty for fun.
"You need my twist; don't be stiff!"
They snorted; both said they were the one.

In the orchard, scents filled the air,
Mandarins whispered sweet delight.
"Let's have a party, if you dare!"
They plotted in the soft moonlight.

Grapefruits grumbled, feeling blue,
"Why so sour?" asked a sprightly lime.
"Let's add some sugar and have a brew!"
And, in jest, they all fell in line.

A splash of fun, a dash of mirth,
In a bowl, they laughed and groaned.
These fragrant pals know their worth,
In zesty circles, mischief is honed.

Sweet & Sour Memoirs

Once a lime had dreams of fame,
To be the zest of the town.
But with each joke, it brought in shame,
"You're just too tangy, sit down!"

A grapefruit shouted, "Hold your rind!
Let's make some syrup, stir it right!
Together we'll shine, and leave behind,
All doubts that we're not a delight!"

Oranges joined with a plucky cheer,
Sprinkling giggles like confetti.
Their memories sweet so called for a beer,
In the kitchen, mischief was ready.

As they stirred in a cauldron of glee,
They savored both sweet and the sour.
Together they danced, so wild and free,
In memories that bloomed like a flower.

Gleaming Citrus Hues

Sunshine bottles on the shelf,
Wiggling, jiggling, bright as a star.
"Taste us all, don't be shy,
We're the party, come as you are!"

Peeling jokes, like oranges rolled,
They bounced and tumbled in gleeful flight.
With every slice, new tales unfold,
Bringing joy from morning till night.

Lemon's kooky hat stole the show,
While lime played tricks like a magician.
All around, the flavors would flow,
In their zany sweet disposition.

So take a sip of that vibrant cheer,
With sparkling smiles that flip and twirl.
Citrus hues, let's spread the flavor,
In this zesty, wild, wacky whirl!

Squeeze of Sunlight

In the morning, lemons grin,
Sunshine spills from chins,
Lime slices dance in the breeze,
Making all the sour freeze.

Oranges giggle in the bowl,
Citrus laughter takes its toll,
Every juice a silly prank,
Eating fruit while sitting plank.

Tangerines roll off the seat,
Dodging feet, what a treat!
Each fruit's got a zesty tale,
Jumps and jives without fail.

With every spritz and splash they sing,
A symphony of zest they bring,
In a world of syrup and sweets,
Fun blooms in every juicy feat.

Citrus Kisses at Dawn

As dawn breaks with a citrus cheer,
Orange marmalade spreads near,
Lemon scones on the table dance,
Making sleepy eyes glance.

A grapefruit blushes in the light,
Claims it's the star of the night,
While limes wear hats of green,
Buzzing like they're kings and queens.

Peeling oranges, what a mess,
Juice spritzes, we're in excess!
With each giggle, spill, and laugh,
Breakfast turns into a craft.

Sipping zest from coffee mugs,
Flavors swirl like happy bugs,
In a riot of fruity bliss,
We start the day with a citrus kiss.

Grapefruit Reverie

In a bowl of grapefruit dreams,
Reality's softer than it seems,
Slicing wedges, bright and bold,
Each segment tells a tale of gold.

Spooned with sugar, sweet surprise,
Tiny halos round our eyes,
Each bite's a cheeky little tease,
Like sunshine wrapped in a breeze.

Silly peels scattered wide,
Who knew fruit could be so spry?
Grapefruit giggles, sings out loud,
'Come on, join this citrus crowd!'

Underneath the morning skies,
Every flavor can arise,
In this juicy, fanciful spree,
We'll laugh and sip eternally.

Peel of Delight

With every twist of zest, we cheer,
The peel launches, oh so near!
Pineapple fumbles, a slippery friend,
Banana rolls like it's on a bender.

Tropical fruits join the party,
Lively tunes being quite hearty,
Peels dance across the kitchen floor,
Sentimentality bursts from their core.

Citrus sprites in a merry whirl,
Snickering as they jump and twirl,
Fruit punch spills, laughter erupts,
Breaking from all the serious corrupts.

This joy in citrus, what a sight,
Happiness in every bite,
As we munch, we can't resist,
The playful charm of the twist!

Zestful Whispers

In the kitchen, a lemon's grin,
Pulls a joke with every spin.
Squeeze it tight, oh what a sight,
Laughter bursts, it feels just right.

Citrus peels with mischief dance,
In a bowl, they take their chance.
Joking fruits, so bright and loud,
Inviting all to join the crowd.

Grapefruits giggle, tangy yet sweet,
Tell the oranges, 'Let's compete!'
They roll and tumble, what a show,
Under sunlight, watch them glow!

With zest and fun, we share a toast,
Celebrating the fruits we boast.
A citrus carnival, what a ride,
In our hearts, the laughs abide.

Lemonade Dreams

Swirls of yellow, oh what a mess,
Splashing sugar, nothing less.
Stirring dreams in a pitcher wide,
Sipping sunshine, come and glide.

Cups are filled, a citrus spree,
A tangy twist, so wild and free.
With every sip, a giggle slips,
Lemonade dreams on frothy trips.

Squirrels join, they start to dance,
Under the shade, in a sunny trance.
Laughter bubbles, a fizzy fall,
Even the ants are having a ball!

A party brewed in every drop,
With playful spirits, we can't stop.
Raise your glass, let's toast the day,
With every sip, we laugh and play.

Orange Blossom Serenade

In a grove where blossoms sway,
Oranges sing, come join the play.
Humming bees in rays so bright,
Create a song, pure delight.

Swaying branches, a fruity tune,
Under the golden afternoon.
Juicy laughter fills the air,
Peeling joy without a care.

A waltz of citrus, bright and bold,
Stories of flavors yet untold.
Chasing dreams on sunlit paths,
As petals dance and citrus laughs.

With every note, a smile ignites,
The blossoms cheer, oh what a sight!
Join the serenade of fun,
When citrus melodies have begun.

Tangy Embrace

A twist of lime, a splash of cheer,
With every bite, the fun draws near.
Juicy tales told with each squeeze,
In a world where laughter's a breeze.

Citrus hugs in vibrant hues,
Peeled back smiles with countless views.
Bouncing flavors, oh what a chase,
Fruits come alive in a tangy embrace.

Mischief bubbles in every bowl,
As sweet aromas captivate the soul.
Lemon meringue, oh what a dream,
Layered laughter like a whipped cream.

With friends around, the fun is clear,
In citrus bonds, we persevere.
Embrace the zest, let laughter flow,
In every moment, let joy grow.

Citrus Harmony

Lemon laughed at the orange's rhyme,
Said, "You're so sweet, it's a citrus crime!"
Grapefruit chimed in with a tart little jest,
"I'm the best breakfast – you all know the rest!"

Together they danced in a bowl of delight,
Squeezing each other, what a silly sight!
Peeling the layers of laughter and fun,
Citrus camaraderie, oh, how we run!

Lime rolled on over, slick as a cat,
"I'm the zest of the party, imagine that!"
Each fruit took turns trying to shine,
Making sure their friendship was fruity divine.

So here's to the gang, fresh and bright,
In the sun's warm glow, a merry sight.
Jokes in the orchard, laughter a must,
In the bowl of happiness, we'll always trust!

Melodic Zest

A tangerine tinny, sang high notes,
While the lemon played tunes on imaginary moats.
Mandarins joined in, with harmony sweet,
Bouncing and twirling on tiny fruit feet.

"Can you hear the rind? It's a jazzy affair!"
Grapefruit grooved on without a care.
"I might be a sour, but I'm still in the game,"
Said the lime with a wink, "it's all just a name!"

Each slice in the sun was a star in the band,
With rhythms that made us all want to stand.
Bouncing and jiving like fruits on a spree,
In this fruity concert, come jam with me!

So pull up a chair, join in the fun,
With a zest for life, let's all be one.
The citrusy chorus, so bright and bold,
Makes every day feel like pure gold!

Sunlit Treasures

In the sunny grove where the fruits all play,
Lemon said, "Let's brighten the day!"
Orange replied, with a vibrant grin,
"Together we'll sparkle, let the fun begin!"

Grapefruit wobbled, a sight to behold,
"I'm the tough one, with a heart made of gold!"
They tossed around laughter like ripe, golden fruit,
Each giggle a treasure, oh, how cute!

A splash of citrus juice, a wink in the air,
Laughter abundant, without a single care.
Each juicy joke brought the sun in our hearts,
In the orchard of fun, where the laughter imparts.

Sunlit treasures, all glimmer and shine,
In a funny fruit world, it's simply divine.
Together we frolic, together we sing,
In this citrus circus, let's crown the spring!

Citrus Pathways

Through the groves of joy, a path fresh and bright,
Citrus travelers walked, what a sight!
"Where to next?" asked the playful lime,
With hopes of adventure, an exciting climb.

Orange declared, "I've got maps in my peel!"
"Follow my trail, it's a zestful deal!"
They rolled past the lemons, laughing with glee,
"The more, the merrier! Come join our spree!"

In the orchard's embrace, they danced side by side,
Every twist and turn, filled with pride.
"Let's make a lemonade stand under the sun!"
Chrickled grapefruit exclaimed, "Oh, this will be fun!"

So onward they ventured, a merry brigade,
With laughter their compass, in sunshine they played.
The path that they traveled, both zesty and bright,
In a world full of fun, everyone's delight!

Orchard of Gold

In the orchard, lemons smile,
Oranges giggle all the while.
Lime trees swing and sway their leaves,
While grapefruits tell the best of peeves.

Bananas trip, they slip and slide,
Fruit salad dreams, nowhere to hide.
Tangerines laugh with fruity cheer,
In the sun, we all persevere.

Sour faces turn to glee,
As sweet juice flows, oh can't you see?
Every nook a burst of fun,
In this grove, we've just begun!

So come and play, let's take a bite,
In fragrant air, our hearts take flight.
We'll juggle fruit and make a mess,
In this orchard, nothing's less!

Juices of Joy

Squeeze the fruit, let laughter flow,
Juices splash; they steal the show.
Pineapple pranks, so very sly,
Bouncing berries as they fly.

Orange peels slip on the floor,
Citrus laughter we can't ignore.
Lemonade storms brew in the glass,
Giggly gazes as we all pass.

Mimosas dance with breakfast plates,
While grapefruit sings, it serenates.
Tasting joy, we never quit,
In our fruity world, we find our wit!

So raise your cup to lemon zest,
For puns and pips, we are truly blessed.
Each sip's a giggle, come share a cheer,
In this juicy land, joy's always near!

Lush Tangle

Through the tangle, fruit trees grow,
Bouncing berries steal the show.
Limes and lemons play in pairs,
As kumquats dance without a care.

Oranges tumble, round and bright,
While grapefruits glow in soft moonlight.
Every branch tells a joke or two,
Fruits unite, creating a crew.

Funny faces on each peel,
Citrus smiles that make us squeal.
In this maze of sweet delight,
Laughter echoes through the night.

So wander through this leafy throng,
In fruity laughter, we belong.
With every twist, we find surprise,
In a world where fun never dies!

Citrus Dance

Under the moon, the fruit friends prance,
Lemons lead in a funny dance.
Oranges follow, in a twist,
As joyous laughter can't be missed.

Limes keep time with zesty beats,
While grapefruits shake on happy feet.
Bananas spin in perfect sway,
As all the fruits join in the play.

Peels are flying, giggles soar,
In this zesty dance, we want more!
Fruity friends create a whirl,
In leafy skirts, we spin and twirl.

So join the fun, don't hesitate,
In this juicy jamboree, it's fate.
With every step, we'll share a laugh,
In our fruity realm, let's craft a path!

Sunbeam Infusion

In the morning, bright and cheery,
I squeeze a lemon, feeling merry.
The zest escapes, a playful dance,
Causing laughter with every glance.

My breakfast plate, a vivid sight,
With orange slices, oh, what a delight!
Each bite bursts forth with sunny cheer,
Turning frowns into smiles near.

Mornings with fruit are such a treat,
Making all my worries retreat.
Just one tangy lick of rind,
Turns my day into a wild unwind!

So here's to fruits, a joyful song,
In every squeeze, I can't go wrong.
With each bright slice and juicy splash,
Life's a party—let's make a bash!

Zesty Embrace

A citrus hug, oh what a thrill,
With every squeeze, I feel the chill.
Lemon drops and limey glee,
In this fruity world, just let it be!

I trip on zest in every way,
Greeting mornings with bright decay.
My shirt? Stained with a citrus kiss,
But every splatter's pure bliss!

The orange gets its chance to shine,
While silly grapefruits toast with wine.
Bantering with tangy friends so dear,
Who needs lemonade? Just grab a beer!

Chasing after scented trails,
My kitchen smells of splendid tales.
So let's embrace this juicy fun,
In our zesty world, we've already won!

Jumbled Juices

In a blender, crazy dreams collide,
Fruits and laughter side by side.
Add a banana, a splash of cheer,
Is it a smoothie, or a fruity beer?

My kitchen's a carnival of taste,
With funky flavors, let's not waste!
Mango mayhem, oh what a scene,
As I concoct this liquid dream!

A sip of chaos, a citrus swirl,
Each gulp brings on a giggling whirl.
Pondered the thought, "What a mix!,"
Syrupy magic in one big fix!

So raise a glass to jumbled fun,
In every drop, let's all outrun.
Keep blending joy, it's quite the spree,
In this zany juice world, I'm ever free!

Slice of Paradise

Peeling back layers with delight,
Discovering gems, oh, what a sight!
Each slice brings sunshine, oh so bright,
In this fruity world, everything's right.

Grapefruit halves like funky hats,
I giggle at my citrus chats.
"Can I wear you?" I jokingly say,
As the zest dances and whisks away!

I serve a bowl of tropic fun,
Laughing as my friends all run.
The pineapple winks, the kiwi grins,
In this paradise, nobody sins!

So let's take a slice, share a laugh,
To juicy moments, let's raise our glass!
With every zestful, cheeky cheer,
In this fruity bliss, we revere!

Radiant Peel

A lemon walked into a bar,
It said, "I'm feeling zesty, ha!"
The lime gave a wink, so sly,
"You're just a fruit, oh my, oh my!"

They ordered drinks with plenty of fizz,
Grapefruit laughed, "This is the biz!"
With every sip, they felt the cheer,
"Let's party, it's our time of year!"

And oranges rolled on the floor,
Spinning tales of yore, oh what a score!
With citrus jokes that made hearts race,
They filled the room with fruity grace.

So if you're down and full of woe,
Just grab a fruit and let it flow!
For laughter's found in every peel,
In this fruity drink, we seal the deal!

Freshly Squeezed Joy

A juicy grape with a wiggly dance,
Says, "Squeeze me, friend, give joy a chance!"
The orange jumped in with a grin,
"Let's twist and shout, let the fun begin!"

The blender roared with frothy delight,
As fruits took turns in a citrus fight.
Pineapple swung, while peach played coy,
Together they brewed a hurricane of joy.

Bottles popped, and smiles appeared,
"Cheers to life!" the fruits all cheered.
With each sip, a chuckle burst,
In this zesty mix, we quench our thirst!

So grab a glass, don't be afraid,
Sip the sweetness that we've made.
Join the fun, don't shy away,
Freshly squeezed laughs are here to stay!

Tart Lullabies

A little lime in a cradle swings,
Sings soft songs of sour things.
"Tickle me sweet with a zesty tune,
Under the sun, we'll dance by the moon!"

Grapefruit giggled, "What a silly fate!"
"Your lullabies can make us late!"
But all agreed with playful shouts,
"Round and round, that's what it's about!"

They rocked and rolled in a fruity dream,
Where every peal became a theme.
With giggles floating on a breeze,
Tart lullabies brought hearts to ease.

So if you hear a citrus lull,
Jump right in, let your heart pull!
For in this world, we're meant to sing,
With every fruit, we share this swing!

Citrus Symphony

A concerto made of peels and zest,
In the orchard, it's a fruit fest!
Lemons strummed on violins bright,
Bananas danced to the moonlight.

Beets looked on, quite confused at best,
"Why doesn't anyone invite me to jest?"
But oranges twirled and said with glee,
"You're rooty! Join our fruity spree!"

The drums were made of bumpy rind,
Together they created a funky kind.
With fruity notes in perfect blend,
The symphony played till the night's end.

So raise your glass and take it slow,
Enjoy the show, feel that citrus flow!
For laughter rings in every note,
In this fruity symphony, we all float!

Juicy Revelations

In a grove where fruits converge,
Lemons talk while oranges surge.
Grapefruits gossip, no time to waste,
And tangerines dance with vibrant taste.

'What's the secret to your zest?'
Asks a lime that's dressed the best.
'It's all in the sunshine, no need to pout,
Just squeeze out the joy, let laughter sprout!'

A lemon said with a wink and grin,
'You can't pick your friends, but you can pick gin!'
Not every sip is sour or sweet,
Sometimes it's best with a twist of beat.

So cheers to the fruits, both big and small,
Each one with quirks that we love most of all.
From puns to punchlines, the juiciest lore,
In this citrus world, who could ask for more?

Tarts and Tales

In a kitchen filled with bright delight,
Citrus treats prepare for a fight.
An orange pie with a cheeky grin,
Proclaims the lemon, 'I will win!'

'Tarts aren't just desserts, they're a sport!'
The lime claimed from his court report.
With buttery crusts and sugar galore,
The battle of flavors we simply adore.

'Watch out!' yelled grapefruit, with a tart little hop,
Lemon meringue whirled and could not stop.
'Who will be crowned the ultimate bite?'
'The sweet might win, but the tang's got the fight!'

In a clash of flavors, they tumbled and rolled,
Stirred up the laughter, arguments bold.
And when they all settled, so happy and bright,
They tasted each other, 'Now that's just right!'

Limoncello Lullaby

Under the stars, the fruits convene,
For a lullaby sweet and serene.
Limoncello's dreams of vibrant rave,
As zestful elves dance and misbehave.

'Close your eyes, don't fret, don't pout,
Just sip on the sunshine and laugh it out!'
Oranges giggle, with a twinkle from gold,
While limes spin tales never told.

A howl from the grapefruit, sharp and spry,
'The night is young, let it fly high!'
In flavors that sparkle and twirl like a kite,
They sing of adventures, from morn until night.

With each citrus note, the world feels right,
A harmony bright, a marvelous sight.
So raise your glasses to fruits we adore,
In this whimsical chorus, who could ask for more?

Orchard Secrets

In the orchard where secrets bloom,
Lemons and limes play peekaboo gloom.
'What are you hiding, oh citrus so sly?'
'Happiness!' replies with a twinkle in eye.

A skit on a tree, the fruits in a line,
Sharing their tales over sips of brine.
'Can you taste the giggles?' a lime boldly asked,
'In every bite, it's a joy unmasked!'

Grapefruit chuckled, 'Oh, what a law!
To keep every joke kept in citrusy awe.
When life gives you lemons, just add some flair,
And watch all your troubles vanish in air!'

So join in the fun, let the laughter ignite,
With zesty surprises that feel just right.
In orchards of whimsy, where fruits sing their song,
The secrets of life are where we belong.

Slice of Radiance

A lemon danced with glee,
In a bowl of fruit, oh me!
Pineapple slipped, what a sight,
Laughter echoes, pure delight.

Orange tried to tell a joke,
But it slipped right off the yolk.
Grapefruit chuckled, rolled away,
Leaving all in bright dismay.

A tangerine wore a bright hat,
To a party, imagine that!
Limes joined in with a zesty grin,
The funny fruit brigade begins.

With every bite, a burst of cheer,
In this fruity world, we persevere.
So slice the radish, toss the sprout,
Join the laugh, there's no doubt!

Rind and Resonance

An orange sang a catchy tune,
With notes that made the blender swoon.
Bananas gathered in a bunch,
Ready for a fruity lunch.

The lime brought puns, oh what a feat,
Juicy humor, ever so sweet.
While grapes just rolled with laughter's thread,
Squeezed tight, like a hug instead.

Did you hear the grapefruit's joke?
It made the oven nearly choke!
Lemons laughed till they turned pink,
Who knew fruit could make us think?

In this orchard, silliness flows,
With every slice, the laughter grows.
From rind to juice, we share a cheer,
A sweet melody that's crystal clear!

Citrus Symphony

In a kitchen bright and grand,
Lemons played in a zesty band.
The oranges jived on the floor,
While the limes called for an encore.

A tangerine, bold with flair,
Wore a tiny scarf, just to compare.
Grapefruit strutted, bouncing high,
A fruity concert under the sky.

The vibraphone was a slicing knife,
Making melodies—a fruity life!
As the blender whirred in key,
The taste buds danced with glee.

This symphony of zest and cheer,
Brings joy to all who gather near.
So, grab a slice and join the tune,
In this Citrus Circus, we'll all swoon!

Sunlit Quench

A glass of juice on the patio,
Sunshine laughs with every flow.
Mango calls, "Come take a sip!"
"Life's better with a fruit-flavored trip!"

Lemons peeked from the sun-kissed vine,
Adding sparkle to our festive dine.
Watermelon showed its sunny slice,
In a world where moments are nice.

Coconuts cracked jokes in the shade,
Their humor's quite a sweet cascade.
Pineapples twirled, danced with flair,
Summertime's magic fills the air.

A toast to fruit, in all its hues,
With every sip, we just can't lose.
So raise your glass, let laughter flow,
In this sunlit quench, let's steal the show!

Grapefruit Glee

In the morning sun, I gnaw,
A grapefruit grin, I draw.
Juicy and bright, a zesty twist,
Who knew breakfast could be this bliss?

A slice of joy, a splash of cheer,
With every bite, I feel no fear.
Life's sour, but I'll take the bold,
Grapefruit giggles bestow the gold.

Wedges dancing on my plate,
Laughing loudly, don't hesitate.
Vitamin C, my jester's crown,
With every squeeze, I won't back down.

Oh, grapefruit, king of smirk and tease,
You're the zing in my morning breeze.
A burst of joy that's grand and free,
A citrus jest, just you and me!

Lemon Drops and Laughter

Lemon drops roll, a sugary thrill,
With a twist of laughter, I can't stay still.
Sour notes in a delightful dance,
Every taste makes my heart prance.

I mix and shake, my kitchen a show,
A sticky mess, oh what a glow!
Zest on my shirt and juice on my face,
Lemonade giggles in this wild race.

Friends gather 'round, with cups in hand,
Lively banter, a citrus band.
Squeeze, sip, ah, sweet jubilation,
Shared joy in every citrus creation!

Through laughter, joy, and some spills,
We toast to life's delightful thrills.
With every drop, we make a sound,
In lemon laughter, love is found!

Summer's Zing

Bright sun above, oh what a scene,
Orange balls rolling, pure and keen.
Picnics, laughter, a sweet delight,
Citrusy smiles in the warm daylight.

Juicy bites, a sun-kissed cheer,
With every slice, we shout "Oh dear!"
Splashing juice, it's all a game,
As citrus fruit brings us fame.

Kids are dancing, a merry whirl,
Like citrus candies, watch them twirl.
Sticky fingers, laughter loud,
In summer's midst, we feel so proud!

Twilight comes, we stay alive,
With zestful tales, our spirits thrive.
As night unfolds, we share the zing,
Citrusy dreams, oh let them sing!

Orchard of Light

In an orchard bright, we play around,
Each plump fruit a giggling sound.
Branches sway with a joyful sway,
Come join the fun, don't delay!

Squirrels scurry, so full of zest,
In this fruity playground, we feel blessed.
Juice drips down, oh what a sight,
It's a carnival of pure delight!

Citron sharers, we peel and laugh,
Creating our wacky, fruity gaffe.
Squeeze the oranges, hear the cheer,
This orchard's magic draws us near.

With every bite, we make new friends,
In this place where laughter never ends.
Under the sun, our spirits fly,
In this orchard of light, oh my!

Citrus Mosaic

In a bowl of fruit, they giggle and sway,
Lemons and limes, in a bright, zesty play.
Oranges wear hats made of funky green leaves,
While grapefruits gossip, as if no one believes.

A slice of a lime, with a wink and a grin,
Claims it's the zest that makes it a win.
The tangerines dance, with a mischievous twirl,
Who knew fruity friendships could cause such a whirl?

A mandarin rolled on a counter so round,
Chasing a lemon, with laughter profound.
Grapefruits sing songs of a citrusy cheer,
While peels sprinkle giggles, spreading joy near.

In the kitchen, the fruits throw an outrageous bash,
Mixing up smoothies with a splash and a splash.
With juice stains on hands and smiles that won't quit,
They toast with their rinds—life's too short to sit!

Citrus Drift

On a breezy day, the oranges took flight,
Floating through clouds, oh what a delight!
A lemon rolled by, looking sharp as a knife,
Claiming adventure is the key to sweet life.

With puffy white clouds as their zesty stage,
Limes tell their tales with a dash of sage.
They twist and they turn, in a dance oh so bright,
Pulling in flavor from morning 'til night.

The grapefruits giggle, making silly old puns,
While lemons trade jokes, counting bright golden runs.
They twirl in the air, like a circus parade,
Not one of them worried about juice that won't fade.

As the sun sets low, the oranges come down,
Wobbling like toddlers, wearing juice for a crown.
With laughter still ringing, in the warm evening air,
They've drifted through fun, what a citrus affair!

Radiance in Rinds

Zesty little wonders, in a colorful pose,
Bright oranges flash in their sun-kissed clothes.
Lemons make linings, so fresh and so bold,
A burst of good humor, never getting old.

Grapefruits debate, who's the juiciest champ?
While tangerines chuckle, lighting up the lamp.
With laughter and brightness, a quaint little crew,
In a world that's sometimes a bit too blue.

They throw a wild party, with peels on the floor,
Mixing up cocktails—who could ask for more?
A lime on the dance floor, showing off moves,
While every fruit drips—yep, everyone grooves!

As night coats the sky, they settle to rest,
Peeled laughter still echoing, citrus confessed.
With rinds full of giggles and joy to rewind,
These fruity companions—what fun life designed!

Lush Lemon Grove

In a grove full of lemons, a ruckus erupts,
Juicy jests tumble, no one interrupts.
The lemons all argue, whose tartness will reign,
While limes join the fray—what a zesty campaign!

A grapefruit shouts, "I'm the king of the blend!"
While oranges giggle, "Let's all make a friend!"
Tangerines snicker, with mischievous cheer,
Making up jokes that are sure to endear.

The branches all sway, their laughter the tune,
While a lemon climbs high, claiming clouds as its boon.
With peels flying wide, like confetti in spring,
A zany lemon fest—oh, what joy do they bring!

When the day comes to end, as the sun starts to dip,
They gather together, a citrusy trip.
With giggles in shadows, and zests in the air,
The lush lemon grove smiles, spreading joy everywhere!

Sunshine in a Peel

A lemon's grin, a bright delight,
Squeezing laughs, oh what a sight!
Oranges giggle, the limes agree,
In this fruity world, we all feel free.

Bananas slip, dance on the floor,
Peels a-flying, who could ask for more?
Pineapples crown each fruity jest,
Tropical laughter, we are so blessed.

Grapefruit chuckles, sweet and tart,
Jokes sprout seeds, a fruity art.
Lemonade showers, smiles in the air,
Sip on sunshine, without a care.

Citrus picnic, a playful spree,
Munch and crunch, just you and me.
Laughter echoes, a juicy cheer,
Squeezed-out giggles, come grab a beer!

Juicy Echoes

In the grove where zesty dreams sprout,
Fruity giggles, we scream and shout.
A tangerine twist, a grapefruit twist,
Oranges dance, can't resist!

Lemons perch with a witty grin,
Poking fun at the din within.
Their zest for fun is hard to beat,
Juicy jokes swirl, a citrus treat!

A lime slips by on a sunny breeze,
Cracking smiles, it aims to please.
Through tangy trails, laughter flows wide,
Fruity companions, let's enjoy the ride!

With every squeeze, a laugh erupts,
As fruits unite in quirky cups.
The juiciest jests take center stage,
In this ripe comedy, we all engage!

Fragrance of Joy

In a kitchen corner, zests collide,
Scent of oranges, sweet and side.
Lemons entice with a fragrant wink,
A zest for humor, let's rethink!

Limes plot mischief, bright and sly,
Rolling around, oh my, oh my!
Tartness tickles, laughter ignites,
As we chop and dice these funny sights.

The kitchen's a stage for citrus plays,
Every fruit shares tales in quirky ways.
In the air, a sweet aroma swirls,
With every giggle, the zest unfurls.

So peel a laugh, let joy take flight,
Fruity frolics, shining bright.
With laughter sprinkled like sugar on top,
The fragrance of joy will never stop!

Orchard's Embrace

An orchard's heart beats bright and cheery,
Lime vines twist as we get all dreary.
Citrus critters join the dance,
Sliding in sync—they've found romance!

Fruity mischief, a whirlwind storm,
Lemonade rivers, keeping us warm.
Kumquats tease, offering the best,
A zesty gathering, a tasty fest!

Oranges swing from tree to tree,
Other fruits join in with glee.
The funny fruit parade, oh what a show,
Bouncing and laughing, go with the flow!

In this orchard, we lose all frowns,
With every ripe wink, we make our rounds.
Juicy joy fills the sunny space,
In the orchard's embrace, let's pick up the pace!

Juicy Echoes

In a land where lemons dance,
Limes forgot their daring chance.
Oranges giggle, oh so bright,
Tangerines roll, what a sight!

Grapefruit jokes they toss around,
Sour and sweet are glory-bound.
Fruit pals gather, full of cheer,
Laughing loudly, let's all hear!

Peeling skins with much delight,
Juicy whispers in the night.
They squeeze out giggles, oozing fun,
Under the bright, warm golden sun!

So let's toast with fruity glee,
Sipping juice, you and me.
In this garden, antics sprout,
Join the laughter, without doubt!

Essence of Sunshine

A hammock's sway with zestful flair,
Lemons lounging, without a care.
Mimosa skies and minty breeze,
All the citrus, if you please!

Fizzy bubbles in the drink,
This fruity world sure makes us think.
Lime popsicle on my nose,
Got a laugh? Yeah, here it goes!

Citrus jigs do tickle toes,
As grapefruit sings in silly prose.
Chasing oranges down the lane,
Silly fruit with no refrain!

Tickling tongues with every bite,
Sunshine squirted, pure delight.
Join the party, bring a squeeze,
Lemonade hugs are sure to please!

Orchard Serenade

In the orchard, fruits unite,
Orange blossoms fly in flight.
Apples grin, they spin around,
Silly sound is all abound!

Banana peels, a slippery chase,
Lemons chuckle in this place.
Pineapples sport a spiky crown,
Join the frolic, don't you frown!

Underneath the leafy shade,
Fruits make plans, their mischief laid.
A band of berries, and they sing,
Jars of jam for everything!

Dancing shoes made of orange zest,
Everyone here feels so blessed.
With each giggle and each cheer,
This orchard sings, sweet and clear!

Citrus Cascade

A waterfall of tangerine,
Squeezed and splashed, oh what a scene!
Lemon lollies in mid-air,
Jumping fruits without a care!

Guava giggles, peachy fun,
Bouncing berries, everyone!
Melon dance with comical flair,
Splashing juice, oh beware!

In this cascade, joy cascades,
Fun and laughter, never fades.
Splashing colors, bright and bold,
Every fruity tale retold!

So leap and frolic, don't be shy,
In the pool where laughter's high.
With every drip of zesty cheer,
Join the splash, bring joy near!

Limoncello Whispers

In a glass, bright and cold,
Lemon dreams unfold.
Sipping on sunshine's glow,
Witty tales start to flow.

Lemon zest flies through the air,
Limoncello's flair.
Dancing like a fruit parade,
Laughs are simply made.

A zestful slip on a sunny day,
Citron antics at play.
Lemons giggle in delight,
Brightening up the night.

So raise a toast to the cheer,
Lemon laughter's here!
With every sip, we propose,
Laughter tickles our nose.

Zestful Heart

A squeeze of joy from citrus trees,
Laughter flowing with the breeze.
Heartbeats rhythm, sweet and bright,
Zesty moments take their flight.

Lemonade spills with a twisty grin,
Tartness hiding in the kin.
Giggles burst from every slice,
Citrus charms that tickle twice.

With every peel, surprises grow,
Puns that citrus always sow.
Zesty jokes, a hearty cheer,
In this fruity atmosphere.

So sip and smile, let rapture part,
Life's too short — zest your heart!
In every drop, let laughter play,
A zesty twist to brighten the day.

Twilight Citrus

As dusk descends, flavors collide,
Citrus laughter, our silly guide.
Grapefruits giggle in a bowl,
Twilight's glow, a zesty stroll.

Limes whisper secrets oh so bold,
Stories of the fruit bowl told.
Under stars, we sip and cheer,
Citrus tales everyone hears.

Oranges roll wagging their peels,
Playing games, testing ideal feels.
With moonlight's kiss on juicy treats,
Everyone dances to fruity beats.

So gather 'round beneath the night,
Citrusy laughter feels just right.
In this twilight, fun's our creed,
Life's a punchline — let's succeed!

Tangy Potpourri

A bowl of zests, so bright and bold,
Fruity giggles, laughter sold.
Tangerine smiles all around,
In this potpourri, joy's unbound.

Chop and mix, a punchy song,
Citrus giggles all night long.
Lime and lemon, friends in crime,
Squeezing laughs — it's fruiting time!

With every bite, the tangy cheer,
Lively spirits far and near.
Citrusy charms in a jolly stew,
Funny moments — all made new.

So let's create a zesty blend,
Where the laughter will not end.
In fruity fun, let's be carefree,
Join the tangy potpourri!

Rind of Inspiration

In a world so bright and frilly,
A chap said, 'Let's make things silly!'
He peeled an orange, quick and spry,
Juice flew high, oh my, oh my!

With every slice, laughter soared,
Citrus jokes, they quickly poured.
What did the lemon say to the lime?
'You zest a whole lot, every time!'

A grapefruit tried to tell a tale,
But ended up with pithy fail.
'Don't peel me now,' it squeaked with fright,
'Let's squeeze some jokes, it feels just right!'

So here's a toast with fruity cheer,
To jokes and giggles, oh so near.
Raise your glass, let's have a blast,
With every rind, fun's unsurpassed!

Aromatic Adventures

In a market buzzing, colors bright,
A fruit stand stood, a wondrous sight.
Lemon's charm was hard to beat,
While oranges danced on their little feet.

'Try this smoothie!' shouted one,
A mix so crazy, it looked like fun.
Pineapple joined, said with a grin,
'Let's blend it up, let the party begin!'

Limes rolled in, wearing shades,
'Life's a zest, let's not be fades!'
They tossed around, made quite a mess,
A fruity brawl, now who would guess?

In laughter loud, they lost all shame,
With squeezy contests, none the same.
So if adventure's what you seek,
Join in the fun, it's all so chic!

Zestful Whispers

In the grove where sunlight beams,
Whispers linger, full of dreams.
Oranges chattered, shared their tales,
Of sunny days and fragrant gales.

A tangerine winked, 'Life's a zest!'
'Grab a friend and join the fest!'
They giggled and rolled, no need for fuss,
'Let's make fresh juice and ride the bus!'

A citrus crew on a joyful spree,
Sipped tangy drinks, feeling so free.
In a twist and turn, the laughter spread,
A pithy pun, 'It's not our bed!'

So when life gets dull, take a cue,
From fruity friends, bright and true.
Whisper sweet nothings, let joy ignite,
In the zest of life, all feels right!

Sun-Kissed Seasons

In springtime's warmth, the fruits do giggle,
With sunny smiles, they dance and wiggle.
A cheeky lemon, sharp and spry,
Called to a lime, 'Come on, oh my!'

In summer's glow, they planned a show,
An orange said, 'Let's give it a go!'
They juggled and laughed, all in good fun,
'Together we shine, like the summer sun!'

As autumn brings a harvest cheer,
Grapefruits gathered, drank local beer.
'Let's toast to us!' with a clink, they gleamed,
In perfect union, all better teamed.

Then winter waved with a chilly breeze,
But citrus friends laughed with such ease.
Even in frost, they found delight,
For fun blooms bright, both day and night!

www.ingramcontent.com/pod-product-compliance
Lightning Source LLC
Chambersburg PA
CBHW070304120526
44590CB00017B/2560

Tapestry of Treasures

A quilt of bright pins sewn into delight,
Each holds a whimsy like stars in the night.
By threads intertwined, oddities dance,
Inviting a chuckle at every glance.

From secrets of friends to odd tales of fate,
These shiny adornments turn laugh into great.
With patterns of history, stitched with a grin,
A tapestry woven where giggles begin.

Legacy in Luster

In a dusty old box lies a gem full of glee,
It sparkles with laughter, yet failed to foresee.
A relic of joy, with a twinkle and jive,
It tells of adventures, where silliness thrives.

Each glint holds a memory, bright in a frame,
With tales so absurd, they echo like fame.
A legacy shiny, wrapped tight with a jest,
An heirloom of humor, forever at rest.

Mementos of Lost Voices

Faded whispers in the air,
Forgotten tales beyond compare.
Laughter dances in the breeze,
Collecting giggles from the trees.

An old shoe with no left mate,
Wonders where it found its fate.
A rubber duck with tales untold,
Swims through memories, bright and bold.

The Brocade of Life's Echoes

Clinking glasses, laughter rings,
In kitchens filled with silly things.
A spoon that sings a tune so sweet,
Tells of meals and dancing feet.

A teapot wears a daisy hat,
While sassy spoons engage in chat.
Echoes jump from shelf to floor,
As pots and pans begin to roar.

Unraveled Secrets in Silver

A glinting pin with stories spun,
Hides secrets of a long-lost fun.
Each curve and twist tells a tale,
Of daring deeds and laughing hail.

A silver fork that once was king,
Swirls in a dance, its bling a fling.
Forgotten gems start to giggle,
As they reveal their ancient wiggle.

Horizon of Heirlooms

In a box of dusty woes,
Laughing socks and tangled bows.
An old map with smudged routes,
Whispers of folly, giggles and toots.

A clock that ticks with a chuckle grand,
Says, 'Hurry up, life's not so bland!'
Snapshots hanging by a thread,
Capture shenanigans once widespread.

Enchanted Elegance

In grandma's box of shiny things,
A frog that dances, a ring with wings.
A charm for luck, a spider's grin,
Whispers of laughter echo within.

Each piece a tale, a lively jest,
A teapot sings, it's quite the quest.
A misfit gem with quite a flair,
Makes all the house cats stop and stare.

Secrets in the Shine

A pendant that holds a cat's meow,
Stories of mischief, lost somehow.
A wink from a pin that seems to know,
The gossip of days long, long ago.

In the shine, secrets dance and play,
Tales of the odd in a quirky way.
A button once bold now wears a frown,
As stories unfold, they tumble down.

The Heart of a Heirloom

A locket that holds a slice of pie,
With whispers of grandma on the sly.
An old cufflink winks, a sneaky tease,
Of wild adventures in a light breeze.

An heirloom's heart beats with delight,
Each thread a giggle, each gem so bright.
The tales of kin, both bold and true,
From faces in silver, they chuckle too.

Reflections in Radiance

A shiny disk that captured light,
Reflects the chaos of folly and fright.
A charm that sings of a far-off place,
Where everyone wears a silly face.

In every sparkle, a joke unfolds,
Past lives of fun, and laughter told.
A whimsical dance in a sunbeam's glance,
Each story sparkles, ready to prance.

Adornments of Forgotten Lore

Once a pin lost its way,
Telling tales of yesterday.
A lady lifted her brow,
"Why are you here, dear old cow?"

With a laugh, it began to hum,
About adventures, oh so fun.
Chasing cats, avoiding dogs,
Here's the tale of silly frogs!

It claimed to date back to Rome,
But really just missed its home.
Each tale got taller, round and round,
But in the end, no truth was found!

Jewels that Speak

A shiny ring with a fat stone,
Gossiping with the silver throne.
"Did you hear what the necklace said?"
"Oh please, it's gone to bed!"

The bracelets rattled in delight,
"Who wears mismatched socks tonight?"
They laughed as proudly they displayed,
Stories in emeralds, well arrayed.

But one lone gem sighed, feeling blue,
"Am I not pretty? What can I do?"
Then diamonds chimed, "Join the fun!"
They winked, "You'll shine when day is done!"

Threads of Time Entwined

A scarf with threads of bright design,
Whispers secrets, oh so fine.
Each stitch a giggle, each knot a prank,
Worn by a wizard, driving the bank!

Socks with stripes laughing aloud,
While trousers form a stylish crowd.
"Did you see what the coat can do?"
"It just ballooned!" said the shoe.

Pants with pockets full of glee,
Holding stories, just for me.
Hats spun tales of lands afar,
Where fashion's wild and dreams are bizarre!

Echoes of Elegance

A hat adorned with peacock's flair,
Spins yarns of love in the air.
Once a crown, it felt so grand,
Now it's lost but makes a stand!

With echoes of laughter it sways,
Recalling all its glory days.
"Remember the dance at the ball?"
"Of course! It almost made me fall!"

Shoes that prance in rhythm bright,
Tripping stars into the night.
Even the lace joins the tune,
Bouncing happily like a balloon!

The Jewelry of Narratives

In a box of trinkets, tales collide,
A worn-out ring with secrets inside.
A brooch of tales, oh, what a sight,
Each gem a laugh, each clasp a bite.

A necklace whispers of dinner pride,
While earrings giggle, they can't hide.
The stories dance like bees in flight,
Jewel-studded humor shining bright.

Stories Woven in Gold

Once a bracelet of shiny flair,
Told of a dance with socks laid bare.
Each link a chuckle, a grin, a shout,
As memories twirl, without a doubt.

A chain of laughter, so snug, so tight,
Holds stories of clumsiness, pure delight.
With sparkle and gleam, they spin and weave,
A comedy quilt, hard to believe.

Charms of Forgotten Fables

Tiny charms, what tales they hold,
A locket once lost, now epic and bold.
A story of sneakers, a trip, a fall,
With giggles and snorts, we recall it all.

A thimble that whispers of stitching woes,
Each snap of the metal, a tale that grows.
The ridiculous moments, like laughter, unfold,
In shiny little trinkets, adventures retold.

Medals of Moments

Winners of chaos hang on a wall,
Each medal shines with a funny sprawl.
The bronze one recalls that epic cake,
A frosting fight, that made hearts quake.

Silver for slipping in socks, oh dear,
Gold for the time we drank root beer.
Each medal gleams with a story or two,
A trophy of laughter, made just for you.

Relics of Reminiscence

In a drawer filled with oddities,
A sock puppet tells tales of my youth.
A rubber chicken plays old melodies,
While my lint collector speaks the truth.

There's a spoon that once stirred tea so grand,
Now it's a trophy of kitchen strife.
In a box, a thumbtack takes its stand,
Claiming it once ruled the office life.

Old postcards hold secrets of love,
Written in handwriting learned in school.
The paper airplanes I proudly shoved,
Still float in my memory pool.

Each token with laughter, each giggle's ring,
A treasure of times that refuse to fade.
Together they form a quirky bling,
Mementos of the joy that we made.

Keepsakes of the Heart

A paperclip bent in an odd shape,
Reminds me of that awkward date.
It twisted and turned like our fate,
   Making laughter a bit late.

A keychain from a place so bizarre,
Where I lost my shoe in a muddy pit.
Now it dangles like a bright star,
   Each jingle echoes my silly wit.

An old ticket from a show so wild,
We laughed when the singer lost their note.
It's the kind of charm no one else compiled,
A badge of friendship, our shared anecdote.

Each keepsake hugs memories tight,
Filling my heart with tales to recite.
But mostly they make me chuckle with glee,
   As I remember who I used to be.

Artifacts of the Unspoken

A crumpled napkin holds sweet secrets,
With ketchup stains of jokes gone wrong.
What happened next is anyone's guess,
   Yet we still laugh about it in song.

Old glasses missing a lens or two,
Claim they once gazed at a falling star.
Now they're the reason for visions askew,
A glorious muse for tales from afar.

A strange hat with feathers, a bit absurd,
   Worn proudly at a silly parade.
It fluffed up my look, stirred quite the word,
   As onlookers cheered unafraid.

Artifacts whisper of funny fights,
Of silly moments and playful plights.
In the gallery of laughter, they'll dwell,
These treasures where joy chooses to swell.

The Necklace of Narratives

A string of pearls, but not too refined,
Each bead a story, each knot a laugh.
One shone bright, while the other's maligned,
Tales of spills that sparked our gaffes.

A charm shaped like a dancing shoe,
That night we twirled and stepped on toes.
Now it reminds me, oh yes, it's true,
That fun trumps elegance, as everyone knows.

A locket that carries an old photo,
Of a cat dressed like a circus star.
We laughed until we couldn't say no,
That memory, now a favorite bazaar.

This necklace, not just threads of old,
But a whimsical tale waiting to unfold.
With each glance, I'm tickled anew,
At the stories that linger like morning dew.

Flickering Memories

In a drawer so deep and wide,
Old trinkets hide, they bide their time.
A fancy ring with a story lied,
Claiming to be a jewel so prime.

A button once bright, now faded to gray,
Claims it won all the dance contests.
But truth be told, in a clumsy way,
It slipped off my shirt during the jest.

A tiny shoe, too small to wear,
Whispers tales of a tiny sprint.
But honestly, it was just a scare,
When I slipped on it, my face did glint.

So take these bits with laughter's grace,
Each item holds a tale so true.
In every nook, we find our place,
Of memories lost and laughter due.

The Gemstone Gazette

Once a necklace of bright green hue,
Swore it was found in the market's glee.
But here's the catch that none once knew,
It fell from a pet, oh woe is she!

An emerald that sparkled, quite divine,
Strangely wedged in a muffin's core.
A tasty treat, with crunch and line,
Not sure what crumbs had been before!

A sapphire blue, with tales of shine,
Said it glowed when you told it jokes.
But every laugh was truly mine,
For it would always hide from blokes!

So gather round the sparkling bling,
Each gem a more hilarious find.
With laughter shared in every ring,
Who knew such treasures could be kind?

Tales of the Twinkling

A pocket watch that lost its race,
Tick-tocked backward, oh what a trick!
It told of time in a comical space,
Losing minutes with every click.

A silver spoon with a bending tale,
Swore it stirred soup with perfect flair.
But every time it set to sail,
It flung the broth and left a glare!

A charm bracelet with jingles loud,
Claims it danced at every fair.
But truth be told, lost in the crowd,
It tangled ropes in utter snare.

So gather 'round, with glee and mirth,
For every piece whispers a jest.
In laughter's glow, we'll find our worth,
With tales that leave us all impressed.

Resplendence of Recollection

A hairpin twinkled like a star,
Claiming fame from a ballroom night.
But really, it fell from a car,
During a chase that felt just right.

A tiny fork from a fairy feast,
Spoke of parties where fairies danced.
But honestly, its charm had ceased,
When someone lost it in a prance!

A locket held secrets far and wide,
Promised romance in each embrace.
But truth was this, with nothing to hide,
It chased a cat and lost the race!

So treasure each shiny, quirky piece,
For memories laugh in the light.
With joy and giggles, let's release,
Our funny tales, pure delight!

Tokens of Timelessness

In the attic lies a shoe,
With tales of a dance or two.
It squeaks and creaks, a funny sound,
Whispers of laughter all around.

A pair of glasses, very thick,
Once worn by a wizard, what a trick!
They magnify the world so wide,
You'd think a giant took a ride!

Old coins with faces, strange and bold,
They jingle tales that never get old.
A pirate's grin, a treasure map,
Or just a kid who loved to nap.

A teddy bear with fur so frayed,
Holds secrets that have never swayed.
Each stitch a giggle, each tear a charm,
It cuddles all fears and keeps you warm.

Designs in the Dust of Ages

A dusty hat upon a shelf,
Claims it once belonged to Elf.
With a feather plucked from a crow,
It tells of adventures we'll never know.

A rusted spoon, its shine now gone,
Stirs up stories from dusk till dawn.
Did it ever taste a meal so grand,
Or remain in silence, a spoon in hand?

A mismatched sock, striped and spry,
Argues it traveled to the sky.
With tales of clouds and bouncing rain,
Now it's hiding in a ball of gain.

A crumpled map with lines askew,
Marks places where gnomes brew.
Each dotted point a punchline told,
Of wonders in a world so bold.

The Pendant of Perspectives

A quirky pendant, shaped like cheese,
Hangs with tales that aim to please.
It spins in circles with each light,
Telling jokes from day to night.

An old keychain, rusted and bent,
Claims it opens the heavens, heaven-sent.
With each jangle a story flows,
Of friendships and laughter that nobody knows.

A locket that's lost its shine,
But holds a secret so divine.
With pictures of clowns and pie-eating men,
It bursts into laughter time and again.

A brooch that looks quite out of sort,
Claims to be from a royal court.
But I suspect it's just a ruse,
Creating stories we can't refuse.

Illuminated Legends

A lantern that flickers, oh so bright,
Claims it lights up the darkest night.
But when you peek inside for a look,
It reveals a tiny fish, a storybook.

A teapot that whistles tunes so clear,
Fables of tea parties, full of cheer.
Whenever it steams, the giggles arise,
With tales of missed cups and silly pies.

A picture frame that's cracked and worn,
Holds laughter sprung from a corner sworn.
Of cats in hats and dogs in shoes,
It tells of fun, of playful views.

A spinning top that never stops,
Dances on tales of treasure drops.
Each twirl a giggle, a wink, a cheer,
A legacy of joy that draws us near.

Gems of the Heart

In the attic sits a shoe,
A creature caught, it won't break through.
My grandma swore it danced at night,
A croaky tune, quite a silly sight.

A watch that ticked, then it tocked,
Gave time away, oh how it mocked.
Once it froze, not a tick to hear,
Even the cat seemed to sneer.

A jingle bell from old St. Nick,
Or was it from a moonlit trick?
It rings when someone starts to sneeze,
Oh, such a noise; it's sure to tease.

Here lie the tales, both wild and sweet,
Life's odd keepsakes, a charming feat.
With every laugh, a memory spins,
Oh, how the heart forever grins!

Radiant Remembrances

A kazoo once lost in the fold,
Squeaked out secrets, tales retold.
At parties, it thought it was a star,
Making melodies, quite bizarre!

A hat with feathers, far too bright,
Wore it backwards, what a sight!
Every fling, a plucky toss,
Lost a feather, felt like a boss.

A spoon that sung when it stirred the pot,
Claimed it could dance; it certainly thought!
In the kitchen, so wild and free,
Stirred up laughter and jubilee.

Memories kept in colorful jars,
Filled with chuckles, laughs, and scars.
Each keepsake a giggle, a prize to hold,
In this treasure chest, pure gold!

Cultured Echoes

A porcelain cat, with a grin so sly,
Watched over guests, oh my, oh my!
It whispered secrets to the mice,
Who danced on the table, quite precise.

A velvet shoe with a tale to spin,
Hobbled along, never quite in.
It chased a dog who fancied a race,
Rolling down the hill, what a face!

A pin with pearls, a fashion faux pas,
Adorned my uncle, who thought he was a star.
Every gathering became a show,
With him on parade, it was quite the glow.

Each quirky keepsake, whispers of glee,
Tickles the toes, sets the mind free.
Echoes of laughter, timeless and dear,
Every tale a gem, bringing cheer!

Past Passions Preserved

A pair of socks, bright pink and blue,
Once a fashion—how they flew!
Dancing up a storm, they were wild,
Bringing giggles, so reviled!

A rubber duck, once full of pride,
Floated in the tub with quite a slide.
A quack that echoed through the hall,
It told the tales of great and small.

An old diary, pages worn,
Gushed of crushes and hearts that mourn.
Every entry, a giggle or sigh,
Resurrecting dreams that never die.

These treasures caught in laughter's grasp,
Moments preserved, a joyful clasp.
With every chuckle, we redefine,
The crazy stories that are divine!

A Cauldron of Colorful Tales

In a pot of glee, stories brew,
Laughter bubbles, oh it's true!
A chicken in a top hat struts,
While a dancing mole just cuts.

Fairies swap fashion tips at night,
While trolls bicker over their height.
A lobster plays piano with flair,
Who knew crabs could dance with such care?

Silly gnomes craft shoes for the mice,
And frogs sing opera, oh so nice!
With tales of wiggle, tales of jig,
Life's a quirky, colorful gig.

In this cauldron, joy overflows,
Every bubbling giggle, it grows.
With stories like sprinkles on cake,
Wouldn't you laugh, for goodness' sake?

Embered Echoes of Existence.

In the hearth of life, stories gleam,
Like smoky whispers, they teem.
A dragon who dabbles in mime,
Leaves everyone laughing in prime.

Ghosts play cards in the dead of night,
With jokes that'd give you quite a fright.
A cat wearing glasses reads a tome,
While mice plan a party at home.

With tales of mishaps and silly falls,
Where clumsy giants dance in the halls.
Each flicker, a laugh, each spark, a grin,
In the embered glow, the fun begins.

So gather around, come join the cheer,
For every chuckle rings crystal clear.
In the warmth of tales, you'll find your place,
Stories glowing, a warm embrace.

Whispers in Metal

In a workshop where shadows play,
Metallic whispers brighten the day.
A spoon tells jokes to a rusty key,
While a mischievous fork climbs a tree.

Nails gossip softly, screws spin a yarn,
Wrenches boast of victory, charm.
A hammer hums a merry tune,
Under the watch of a silver moon.

A bell rang out with laughter enclosed,
As tongs and ladles spun around, dozed.
Among the tools, stories collide,
Inside this garage, fun's bona fide.

So listen close to the whispers dear,
In the clink of metal, joy draws near.
Every grin, each twinkle of light,
Crafts a world of laughter each night.

Tales Woven in Gold

In a realm where the glittering tales mingle,
Golden threads loop and jingle.
A cat in a crown, regal and sly,
Invites all creatures to swing by.

Bees in tuxedos dance with flair,
While butterflies wear jewels, if they dare.
A fish in a bowl plays charades,
With tales of treasure, escapades.

With every stitch, a story shines,
Of giggling unicorns and playful lions.
These woven tales, a fabric of cheer,
Crafting a world where humor's clear.

So marvel at the golden embrace,
Where laughter and mischief find their place.
For in each tale, bright and bold,
Is a secret of joy, wrapped in gold.

The Art of Memory

In a drawer full of trinkets, lies a shoe,
It reminds me of my dance with a ghost named Lou.
We slipped and slid on a floor made of cheese,
Laughing so hard, we brought cows to their knees.

A spoon with a tale of a soup gone awry,
My cousin declared, 'I could cook it, oh my!'
But the pot exploded, sending peas everywhere,
And the dog took a bath, while we gasped in despair.

A hat with a feather from a bird who could sing,
Added flavor to every silly, joyful thing.
In the midst of laughter, the stories unwind,
Each memory sparkling, unique and refined.

So here's to the moments, both silly and bright,
Condensed in small objects, like stars in the night.
With every small token, a giggle, a grin,
A reminder that life's just a comedy spin.

Gemstone Chronicles

A sapphire ring worn by a sly old crow,
Claiming it glowed when he danced in a show.
Each flap of his wings brought a raucous cheer,
But he slipped on a banana, and flew in sheer fear.

Emeralds once whispered of a prancing cat,
Who thought he was suave, but fell flat like a mat.
He strutted so proud, on the fence made of wood,
Till a sneaky raccoon shared his 'fashion' for good.

Topaz we laughed at, with a joke so absurd,
It tickled our earlobes, not a single word heard.
As we chuckled and guffawed at the shiny, bright light,
Our friendships grew stronger, like gems in the night.

In the chest of delights, stories glitter and spin,
Each facet a memory, where laughter begins.
With every odd trinket, a smile to recall,
A treasure of tales, the best gems of all.

Captured Moments in Silver

A silver spoon with a story so grand,
Once stirred my tea with a mischievous hand.
It slipped through my grasp, danced on the floor,
And knocked over cookies, oh, what a score!

A forgotten locket with photos inside,
Of a cat that once wore a dazzling slide.
He tumbled and rolled with a flick and a spin,
And got himself stuck in a box with a pin.

A tiny bell jingled with every good deed,
But rang when I tripped over my own two feet.
The echoes of laughter, as I sprawled on the ground,
Made even the flowers laugh hard and profound.

So here's to the silver, oh how it shines bright,
Reflecting our memories, so silly, so light.
In this treasure of past, we find joy and glee,
Captured forever, like leaves on a tree.

Hidden Narratives

In a dusty old chest lies a tale of a shoe,
That danced with a squirrel wearing a hat made of blue.
They twirled at the moonlight, a sight so divine,
Until they both tripped on a spaghetti vine.

A tiny old mirror, full of charms and quirks,
Reflects all the secrets of dancing with jerks.
I grinned and I giggled, at the faces I found,
Each silly expression made joy abound.

A necklace of buttons from shirts long ago,
Spoke of adventures, both silly and woe.
Each button a chapter, with threads all askew,
Narratives tangled like yarn in a zoo.

So here we sit laughing, with stories to share,
In a world full of trinkets, each with a flair.
Hidden and shining, like treasures anew,
These moments of madness connect me and you.

Life's Glimmering Narrative

In a world of shiny tales,
Old socks dance in grand parades.
Mismatched buttons tell of fails,
Each accident cleverly aids.

A cat in a top hat sings,
While roosters scheme from their perch.
Legends of tangled strings,
Make the dull laugh and lurch.

Lemons wearing fuzzy hats,
Spin gossip under the sun.
Dancing shoes on friendly rats,
Chasing fun like it's a run.

Tall tales dressed in vivid hues,
Like jellybeans worn as crowns.
In laughter, we find our muse,
Shining bright in silly towns.

Bejeweled Whispers

A pineapple plays chess with glee,
While olives gossip with delight.
Curly fries climb a leafy tree,
Creating stories through the night.

Each twinkling star is dressed in flair,
Whispering secrets to the moon.
A fish in boots, without a care,
Recites its waltz, a comical tune.

Socks play hopscotch, what a sight!
With marbles rolling down the lane.
Balloons engage in silly fights,
While cupcakes flaunt their frosted gain.

Giggling shoes tap on the floor,
Crafting chaos as they play.
In the laughter, there's much more,
Stories shine in a quirky way.

Enigmatic Embellishments

A snail with pearls, full of flair,
Joins the frogs in witty games.
They leap with grace, without a care,
Dressed in laughter, not in names.

Jellybeans plot a sweet escape,
As candy canes form a brigade.
With gummy bears in capes,
Silly escapades, well displayed.

Funky hats on heads so wild,
Bouncing thoughts like popcorn popped.
Each riddle held by a bright child,
Makes even the frowns be dropped.

Jokes encrusted in sunshine gleam,
Twirling tales from fridge to sky.
In whimsical whispers, we dream,
Where giggles bloom and stories fly.

The Weight of the Past

Old shoes tell stories of long walks,
Through puddles, mud, and funny trails.
Hats with quirks hold silent talks,
Of wild parties, jiggly scales.

Timeworn teacups spill their tea,
Recounting love in fuzzy threads.
With sassy spoons, they giggle free,
While the kettle clinks on reds.

Dusty books whisper to the breeze,
Chapters of all that once was fun.
Tales of dandelions and bees,
Murmurs travel, never done.

Beneath it all, the laughter glows,
In silly joys that we embrace.
The stories old with love still flows,
Weighty yet light in every space.

The Charm of Chronicles

In a dusty drawer I found it,
A tiny tale in silver thread.
It giggles and whispers secrets,
Of socks that never found their bed.

A button that danced on its own,
Claiming rights to the sock's lost mate.
It swayed with grace, unabashed,
In a kingdom where laundry can wait.

A thimble with dreams of the seam,
Wishes stitched in every crease.
What tales it could spin, it seems,
Of a tailor's cat that caused a mess!

Now I wear it, a storyteller bold,
Here's to laughter and years gone by.
Each glance at this charm unfolds,
A laugh, a giggle, and a sigh!

Heirlooms of Heartstrings

A locket that once held a cat's face,
Clutched tightly through many a night.
It purred every time it was placed,
On the collar of a shirt so tight.

Grandma's old shoe, a relic of strife,
Still holds the smell of her spice rack.
Its sole knows the hustle of life,
Tap-dancing down memory's track.

A spoon that once stirred a stew,
Now sits solo with tales to tell.
Of epic feasts, recipes new,
And a mix-up involving jelly and gel.

So here's to the odds and ends,
That remind us to smile and play.
In laughter, our heartstrings blend,
Creating stories each day!

Petals of Memory

A flower pressed in a dusty book,
Holds secrets of summers gone.
It giggles as I take a look,
Reminds me of the ice cream con.

Each petal tell tales of joy,
Of little hands crafting a crown.
A prince made from mud, oh what a boy,
While sister claimed the royal gown.

A bee buzzed in, with too much flair,
And the crown fell, chaos ensued.
Laughter mixed with shouts in the air,
As nature mocked our royal mood.

Now in frames, their stories remain,
A testament of laughter and breeze.
In petals of memory, the mundane,
Turns magical with such ease!

The Memoir in Gems

A sparkling ring once lost by Dad,
Claimed by the dog who chewed it raw.
He wore it proudly, not a bit sad,
As the family erupted in guffaws.

A necklace of pearls, faux, no less,
That Auntie wore to the dance for fun.
It tangled up after a bit of stress,
And turned into a saucy bun!

Eyes can't believe the sights they see,
When each gem has stories to share.
A chirp, a chuckle, as wild as can be,
In heirlooms that polish the air.

So every shine has a cha-cha beat,
Each laugh ripples through the years.
With gems that twinkle, oh so sweet,
The memoirs sparkle amidst our cheers!

Fragments of Memory

In the attic, dust bunnies play,
Old hats hide secrets from yesterday.
A mismatched sock laughs on the wall,
Whispers of laughter echo through the hall.

Grandma's shoes still know the dance,
While rogue spoons dream of a chance.
The teapot spills tales of tea,
Each cup a chapter, wild and free.

A broken clock ticks out of tune,
Yet time, it waltzes, a lively boon.
Forgotten toys, their stories collide,
Adventure awaits, oh what a ride!

In each corner of this quaint space,
Memories twirl in a clumsy grace.
A comedy of errors, all on display,
Oh, how these fragments love to play!

Adornments of Time

A crooked hat sits atop the shelf,
Once a dandy, now just itself.
Brooches whisper in jumbled tones,
Gossiping gently like old-time phones.

A tie-dye scarf from the '70s days,
Makes fashion statements in quirky ways.
Button collections, a wild parade,
These little gems take center stage.

A calendar full of crossed-out plans,
Hiding new thrills in the gaps and spans.
The fridge hums tales of leftovers sweet,
While magnets at attention compete.

Polka-dot pajamas tell of late nights,
When laughter erupted in whimsical flights.
Each trinket a tale, absurdity's muse,
Life's funny fragments, we gladly excuse!

Tapestry of Tales

Woven threads of laughter and cheer,
An old rug spills stories, my dear.
Mice in the walls giggle with glee,
As quirkiness dances, wild and free.

A costume chest bursting at seams,
Outfits that sparked forgotten dreams.
A pirate's hat and a tutu bright,
Fashion faux pas, oh what a sight!

A painting askew, with paint splotches bold,
Each drip a tale waiting to be told.
Chairs creak with stories from long ago,
Of guests and feasts that stole the show.

Underneath the stairs, shadows prance,
Imagination's realm where specters dance.
This tapestry hums with whimsical schemes,
Crafted from laughter and childhood dreams!

Echoes in Embellishment

Decorations hide in playful delight,
Laughing out loud in the soft twilight.
A tinsel crown that once was so grand,
Now draped on the cat, she takes a stand.

Confetti from parties, it snickers away,
As it dreams of dancing in a parade.
Balloons filled with stories of parties unplanned,
Float in the corner, a goofy band.

Painted rocks whisper under the sun,
Each one a character, oh what fun!
A seashell that plays ocean's old song,
Echoes of laughter where all belong.

With ribbons and trinkets, the room's alive,
Where whimsical treasures laugh and thrive.
An ensemble of quirks, loud and bright,
In embellishments echoing sheer delight!

Histories in the Halo

A flamingo in a tuxedo, quite the sight,
Bobbing to music in the pale moonlight.
He winks at the crowd, causing quite a stir,
With tales of dust bunnies and rogue fur.

A ladybug strutting in sparkling shoes,
Shares tales of spilt tea and dance floor blues.
Her stories, a riot, make all giggle loud,
While crickets take notes, feeling quite proud.

A cat in a top hat, juggling some fish,
Whispers of dreams, and a long-lost wish.
His antics provoke uncontrollable glee,
As we ponder the deep, or just sip our tea.

Beneath the wild tales, there's mischief and cheer,
Each laugh a reminder, to hold what's dear.
For even the sillies weave threads so divine,
In the halo of laughter, our stories entwine.

Carvings of Time

The cactus holds secrets, true and absurd,
It witnessed the dance of a very loud bird.
Each groove tells of martinis and love,
And how one lost rollerblading glove.

A snail with a shell, all fancy and bright,
Unraveled the tales of a wiggly flight.
He claims he once raced with a tortoise bold,
But ended up stuck in a sink, truth be told.

A mushroom once sighed, its cap oh so wide,
Listened to ants with nowhere to hide.
They laughed of their trips, on a crumb-filled spree,
While dodging the pigeons watching with glee.

The carvings in wood, the whispers of air,
Craft stories that surge like a whimsical flare.
With each sip of nonsense, we'll gather and toast,
To the humorous trails that we cherish the most.

The Weight of Memory

A squirrel recalled chasing a runaway hat,
While slipping on acorns and dodging a cat.
With every hop, he laughed, just a bit,
Recalling how branches he'd once proudly split.

An old shoe on a fence shared tales of the past,
Of puddles and romps, a yearning so vast.
It sighed of a soul who once danced with the rain,
Now merely a relic, yet never in vain.

A teacup remembered a clumsy ballet,
Where tea leaves twirled in an elegant fray.
Even chipped, it exclaims, 'Oh, I'd do it again!'
For memories fluff like clouds in the rain.

Each memory weighty, yet light as can be,
Bringing joy and laughter, as sweet as a spree.
With stories that float on the front porch swing,
We'll gather the moments, oh what they bring!

Glamour and Grit

A penguin in pearls, slipping on ice,
Flashing a grin that's simply precise.
He twirled and he leaped, saying, 'Look at me!'
While the polar bears watched with a chuckle of glee.

A dog in a bow tie, ready to mingle,
Sipped from a fountain, let out a jingle.
With tales of the mailman, mad antics galore,
Made friends with the squirrels who knotted a score.

In the midst of the chaos, a chicken in heels,
Told of a world made of fanciful reels.
With glamour in feathers and grit in the heart,
Every step she took, a rebellious art.

So let's raise a toast, with stories to share,
Of glamour and grit, and abundant flair.
For in laughter and joy, we find our sweet wit,
Echoed in moments of chaos and grit.

Celestial Charms

A star fell down, but what a sight,
It landed soft in my cat's night fright.
He chased it 'round, with a pounce and a leap,
While I just laughed, and tried not to weep.

A comet's tail tangled in my hair,
My friends now swear I dance on air.
With each twirl, a giggle breaks free,
They say I'm the cosmos, can't you see?

The moon winked once, I took it to heart,
My jokes now land like a shooting star.
I tell tall tales, while they roll their eyes,
But laughter floats up, into the skies.

So bring your stars, and meteorite shoes,
Together we'll dine, with laughs as our muse.
In this celestial ball, we find our way,
With funny charms that make dull days sway.

The Essence of Memories

I found an old hat with stories galore,
It belonged to my granddad, who danced on the floor.
With each twist and turn, he leapt with such grace,
I'd join him in spirit, just to keep pace.

A pair of shoes, once shiny and bright,
Now tell of adventures, from morning 'til night.
They've seen muddy puddles and squeaky clean floors,
A legacy tangled in laces and boars.

An old photograph, what a comedian's pride,
With hair like a lion, and laughter inside.
Each snapshot reveals a hilarious tale,
Of road trips and mishaps, too funny to fail.

So wear the past's jewels, let laughter ignite,
In this whimsical dance, we'll shine ever bright.
With memories woven, like fabric of cheer,
Let's tickle the fancies of those we hold dear.

Stories at the Edge of a Pin

A silver pin rests, holding tales untold,
Of jellybean dreams and adventures bold.
It sparkles and twirls, in a wink of an eye,
Transporting us all, to where giggles fly.

A button once failed, but now it's a star,
In fabric of laughter, we've stitched it afar.
With each tiny poke, stories assemble,
A patchwork of joy, as memories tremble.

A needle of humor stitches us tight,
As we laugh off blunders and jokes in the night.
On fabric of moments, we dance on a pin,
With each bustling stitch, let the fun begin!

So gather your treasures, come join in the fun,
With laughter as glue, and friendship outrun.
At the edge of a pin, there's a world waiting still,
Where stories unite, and humor we will fill!

Adorning Ghosts of the Past

In grandma's trunk, I uncovered delight,
A ghostly ensemble that danced in the night.
With costumes and tales that tickle and tease,
They whisper in giggles, a world meant to please.

A dancing pair of shoes with a mind of their own,
They shuffle and bop, while I sit alone.
A round of applause for the spirits that play,
They've twisted their way through the laughter of days.

An old necklace jangles, with whispers of yore,
Each bead tells a story of laughter and more.
With a chuckle and snicker, they echo the past,
In a fabulous frolic that's meant to last.

So let's put on costumes and dance with the ghosts,
With humor as our guide, we'll celebrate hosts.
Adorning our memories, where giggles abound,
In the hearts of our stories, true joy can be found.

Narratives in Natural Beauty

In the garden, where weeds laugh,
A daisies' dance brings a photograph.
Bumblebees wear tiny hats,
And gossip with the nimble chitchat.

The sunflowers wave, a soft hello,
While squash plants throw a showy glow.
Ladybugs don their polka dots,
As caterpillars tie up their knots.

A squirrel spills secrets on the grass,
As butterflies gather for the class.
Nature's circus, such a sight,
Where each moment is pure delight.

With laughter sewn in petals bright,
Every bloom holds stories tight.
So join the creatures, let them share,
The tales of mischief floating in the air.

Forgotten Fables in Fusion

Once a fish dreamed to fly high,
But his fins could only wave goodbye.
He wore a hat of seaweed green,
A cap that made him feel quite keen.

A crab told tales of underwater cheer,
Of jellyfish that threw a grand frontier.
Stingrays danced with elegant glee,
While octopi played hide-and-seek in spree.

Turtles strolled with stories bold,
Cherishing treasures of tales retold.
With every wave, their laughter grew,
In depths where forgotten fables grew.

So raise a shell and dive in deep,
Where fish still dream and crabs still leap.
Each splash a giggle, every wave a cheer,
In this watery world, we hold so dear.

A Glint of Retrospectives

In an attic full of dusty shoes,
A pair once danced with vibrant hues.
They twirled with socks and a tin can,
Creating a waltz, oh what a plan!

A forgotten bear in a tattered coat,
Dreamed of sailing on a rickety boat.
He recited poems to the moths,
While they reminisced, all covered in cloths.

Old records whispered songs of yore,
As vinyls echoed, seeking more.
Each scratch and skip held laughter bright,
Replaying stories in the soft moonlight.

So raise your glass to moments passed,
To quirky memories that ever last.
In every shadow, there's fun to find,
A glint of joy for the heart and mind.

Stories Within the Stone

A pebble claimed to be a sage,
With wisdom gathered through every age.
It spilled its tales with such finesse,
Of creatures, myths, and foolishness.

Once a boulder with a heavy frown,
Dreamed of dressing up like a crown.
But rocks don't move, so it stayed still,
A comedian, with laughter to fulfill.

In the gravel, a curious chat,
Mixes with gossip from the brave old rat.
And every crack holds a secret bloom,
Whispering stories from the earthen gloom.

So lift a stone, give it a shake,
Maybe it holds a tale to break.
For in each grain, we find a jest,
And humor lives where nature's blessed.

Messages from the Past

In a drawer full of dust, I find,
A love note written, oh so blind.
It claims I'm clever, witty, and rare,
Yet I can't recall, was this a dare?

A old sock puppet, no match for me,
Sad eyes that beg for a cup of tea.
In the attic it wails a fuzzy tune,
Outlived its purpose, yet still a boon.

A grandpa's tie that twists and sways,
Holds tales of clumsy, unglamorous days.
It danced with the raindrops, twirled in a breeze,
Now it just hangs and dreams with ease.

A rubber chicken, quite out of place,
Waving frantically with its silly grace.
Each squeak recalls a laugh from the past,
A chuckle lives on, and it always will last.

The Art of Frivolous Reminders

My fridge is adorned with notes and more,
A reminder to buy, even cake to store.
But who wrote 'Coffee!' in vibrant pink ink?
Did I think I'd forget? Well, what do you think?

A shiny button claims that it's wise,
Telling me all that I should despise.
But what if I'm blind to its judgmental sneer?
Shiny objects can't share a true rapport here.

A sticky note, weathered and torn,
Whispers of breakfast and how to be reborn.
Yet it lists things like 'dance by the moon',
Was I meant to waltz? I hope not too soon.

The coffee mug with a handle so wide,
Holds secrets of spills and dreams that've died.
With phrases of comfort, it offers a cheer,
To forget all the nonsense, and sip without fear.

Story-draped Trinkets

A keychain of whales, oh so absurd,
More of a joke than wise, I've heard.
Yet it reminds me of that trip gone wrong,
When a whale sang notes, oh that silly song.

A tiny bell hangs, but who knows where?
Ringing in laughter from layers of air.
Did it chime when joy was at its best?
Or was it a joke on a dare from the jest?

A broken compass lies under the bed,
Claiming it leads to the place we dread.
It spins around as if it's got flair,
But goes nowhere, just plays with the air.

A glittery shoe lost from a dance,
It dreams of bright lights and one last chance.
But here it rests, covered in dust,
Longing for rhythm and a twirl of trust.

The Glisten of Legacy

A pocket watch, paused at a certain time,
Holding the moments of love and a rhyme.
But do I dare wind it? What would it say?
Is life a tick-tock or just a buffet?

An old spoon whispers tales at the table,
Of meals that were shared, and gossip so fable.
But its shine's now dulled, a trifle, a joke,
Was there ever a feast or did we just poke?

A collection of buttons from suits of the past,
Representing fashion, fading so fast.
But each has a story, quirky or grim,
Buttoned up memories on a very short whim.

A dusty old hat wearing history's grin,
Just sits on a shelf, with dust layers thin.
Yet it winks at the stories that spark in the night,
Leaving a trail of laughter, pure delight.

Timeless Trinkets

A button here, a clasp gone,
Caught in a time travel yawn.
Each piece has a tale to tell,
Like a cat that thinks it's swell.

Old watch hands spin in delight,
Ticking tales of day and night.
A mismatched earring, oh what fun,
It thinks it's paired, but it's just one!

A thimble's dance in a grand parade,
Telling secrets that never fade.
Those glasses are half-full with cheer,
Promising fun will always be near!

A paperclip in a fancy dress,
Winks at us, "I only impress!"
With each shiny glimmer, we laugh,
For these tiny tales are quite the craft!

Fables in the Fragments

A locket whispers a gossipy tune,
Of lovers caught under the moon.
A pin with a tale of lost socks,
Twirling in mishaps like silly clocks.

An acorn cap, a crown for a mouse,
Holds the gossip of the whole house.
A tiny spoon sings of soup so grand,
Imagining feasts in a make-believe land!

A broken ring tells of silly fights,
When 'stupid' replaced 'goodnight, goodnight.'
Each piece holds joy in its own way,
Crafting giggles in bright array.

The fabric of life is stitched with glee,
Every stitch a tale, so let it be!
A story of laughter is never too far,
In a world filled with glittering memoir!

Mementos of the Heart

A rubber band that held dreams tight,
Flung away in a reckless flight.
A lost clip sings of a style of old,
In the corner with memories bold.

A penny worn, a wish so grand,
To buy a laugh in a far-off land.
A charm from a cotillion night,
Twirled through parties, oh what a sight!

Forgotten key, what door did you find?
Unlocking giggles that rewind.
A stray button hides in a shoe,
Pretending it's a gentleman too!

The heart collects these pieces rare,
Locking humor in moments to share.
Like fireflies caught in a jar,
Each memory twinkles, each one a star!

The Sparkle of Legends

An old coin with an emperor's frown,
Spinning tales of fortune and crown.
A toy soldier, proud and spry,
Winks at the tales as they fly by.

Another charm, a dancing bee,
Buzzing through tales of jubilee.
A nutcracker dressed to impress,
With laughter, he'll surely bless!

A feathered quill writes legends anew,
With giggles and dreams painted in blue.
A piece of string, oh what a tease,
Wraps around moments with effortless ease!

Together they twinkle, a joyful band,
Unfolding tales across the land.
These playful fragments of time and whim,
Sparkling bright, never quite dim!

Each Layer a Tale

Once I found an old pin, so grand,
Its tales seemed to dance, hand in hand.
A cat and a hat fought in glee,
Tales wrapped in laughter, wild and free.

Each layer a story, quite absurd,
Of biscuits that sang and trees that blurred.
A grandma with secrets, quite the tease,
In her tales, nothing was as it seems.

With a wink and a nod, the stories unfold,
Of nights bathed in glitter and pockets of gold.
A dragon who chirps, under moonlight's gleam,
In this merry grand tale, nothing's as it seems.

So slide it on gently, let laughter erupt,
A pin full of whimsy, joyfully plumped.
With every small gleam, a chuckle or two,
A treasure of stories, all just for you.

Past Polished in Gemstone

In a drawer where the old treasures hide,
Lies a bauble, a spark, a gleaming pride.
Each facet a giggle, each shimmer a laugh,
Stories of mischief, with a fun little gaff.

A wobbly penguin, who danced with flair,
And a snail that delivered the gossip somewhere.
Every scratch tells a joke, every dent hums a tune,
In this polished gem, nonsense's a boon.

With jingles of laughter, it jingles along,
Mocking the serious, flaunting the wrong.
The past wraps around, like a patchwork embrace,
Animating tales with a sparkling grace.

So wear it with glee, let it swing and sway,
A piece of the past, colored wild like a play.
In gemstones we're stuck, but always in jest,
Where warmth meets the funny, and laughter's the best.

Whispers of Worn Stories

A trinket of whispers, soft and light,
Holding secrets of giggles, hidden from sight.
It chirps of a squirrel, well-versed in schemes,
And a dog wearing socks, pursuing its dreams.

In corners it chuckles, with stories to share,
Of owls who do yoga, in the cool evening air.
A rabbit in bunny slippers, oh so spry,
Decreeing that snacks are the best reason why.

With every rub, tales tumble and swell,
Of fumbles and tumbles, all worked out so well.
It spins you a yarn that's both funny and warm,
Where laughter's the breeze, in every sweet storm.

As you pin it on, take a chance, take a laugh,
A brooch of delight, a whimsical craft.
In whispers it glimmers with tales of delight,
Bringing smiles and chuckles, every day and night.

Ties that Bind

In this curious pin, stories get jiggy,
Of friendships and blunders, all quite the giggy.
A cat with a shoe, and a cake that won't stop,
Each tale a deliciously tumble-filled drop.

Knots that are tangled, but woven with care,
Of moments that sparkle, like jewels in the air.
A bear in a tutu, spinning around,
With ties that bind laughter and joy all around.

The stories are silly, yet precious they cling,
Of hats that fly high and frogs that can sing.
With a wink from the past and a nod from today,
These ties are the threads that keep worries at bay.

So wear it with pride, let fun be your muse,
In this wild little tale, there's nothing to lose.
The laughter's not shy, it shouts loud and clear,
Worn close to the heart, bringing joy ever near.

A Collection of Wandering Memories

In the attic, dust bunnies play,
Whispers of yesteryears sway.
A sock that once had a match,
Now dreams of adventures to catch.

A photo of cats in a hat,
Waiting for a gig, imagine that!
A rubber chicken, so bold and bright,
Arguing with a flashlight at night.

Forgotten tales in an old drawer,
Where mismatched socks start to roar.
A cup that claims to grant wishes,
But only brews cold coffee dishes.

Each memory dances, a silly sprite,
In a world where laughter takes flight.
These snippets of life, a grand parade,
In the play of absurdity, we wade.

The Lattice of Lore

A legend of pants that refused to fit,
Made a daring escape, oh what a skit!
A tale of ice cream that vanished too,
Only to find out it fell in a shoe.

Oh, the capers of socks on vacation,
Each one seeking its grand destination.
A fork that wanted to be a spoon,
And sings little ballads 'neath the moon.

A hat that once danced with a broom,
Chasing away all the impending gloom.
The wisdom of goldfish—quite profound,
Who think their bowl is the whole wide ground.

Listen closely to the stories spun,
In tangled yarns where laughter's begun.
The web of giggles and quirky bites,
A lattice woven in whimsical nights.

Threads of the Past

A scarf that met a toaster one day,
Exchanged tales of warmth in a playful way.
A thimble that dreamed of being a star,
With needle and thread, it ventured far.

In the corner, a shoe with a flair,
Claims it once danced with a teddy bear.
The buttons all chatter, gossip in threads,
Of secrets shared in the quiet of beds.

A paperclip, bold, tries to fly,
But ends up hanging on, oh my!
Each stitch and each fiber, a chuckle inside,
Woven with joy, in laughter we ride.

From knitting disasters to crafty delight,
These threads of the past keep us light.
With colorful tales that never quite cease,
In fabric and fun, we find our peace.

The Mosaic of Unwritten Words

In a jar of jellybeans, stories collide,
Of heroic pickles and jellybean pride.
A pizza slice plotting a silly scheme,
To swim with the fish in a ketchup dream.

A diary filled with drawn-out doodles,
Of cartoon ducks and dancing poodles.
Each silent page a canvas so grand,
Where laughter's erupted by whimsical hand.

Vocabulary fragments, all jumbled and free,
Compose a chaotically happy spree.
A mystery wrapped in a riddle quite sly,
Guess the punchline and watch giggles fly.

In this mosaic of rich little whims,
Laughter's the rhythm, and joy often swims.
We dance through the words, both funny and fun,
Scribing tales of delight 'til the day is done.

Sagas in Small Settings

In a teacup, a dragon snored,
While the sugar cubes formed a horde.
Did you hear the cookie's tale?
It galloped off, a brave morale!

A cat in a hat brewed some tea,
For the mice who danced in glee.
A noodle slyly jumped for joy,
Claiming to be the world's best toy!

A chipmunk painted stripes on the wall,
While a pickle played a wooden ball.
In corners, the dust bunnies pranced,
While a donut twirled, entranced!

The spoons whispered stories of yore,
Of pirates who lived behind the door.
Each item spoke of mischief and glee,
In this tiny world, full of spree!

History in Brilliant Hues

A purple elephant danced on a beam,
Like a character straight from a dream.
The crayons giggled with vibrant cheer,
As the paper sighed, not near a smear!

A royal blue fish wore a crown,
While a polka-dot chicken sang in town.
Their gossip painted the sky with flair,
Each color a giggle in the air!

The yellow sun tickled the grass,
While flowers in pink dared to sass.
In this patchwork tale of delight,
Funny shadows danced in the light.

The laughter span from brush to pen,
While the rainbow's end whispered "Do it again!"
Once upon a hue, bold and bright,
History twinkled through laughter's light!

Lost Launchings of Luster

A rocket made of shiny tin,
Tried to blast off with a goofy grin.
But it rolled down the hill instead,
Back to the launchpad where kittens tread.

With a bang and a fizz, the toast did fly,
While the bread lamented, oh so shy.
Butter bugs led a grand parade,
On a sandwich slice, a balmy cascade!

A traffic cone wearing a cape,
Dreamed of being something great.
But it tripped on a pebble, oh dear,
Spinning stories for all to cheer!

Thus laughter soared in the funny skies,
With lost launches catching bright eyes.
Every hiccup, a jolly charm,
In the tales of whimsy, safe from harm!

The Symphony of Stones

The pebbles formed a rock band,
With a tiny conductor waving his hand.
A smooth stone sang like a bird,
While the gravel joked, quite absurd.

A boulder stomped with heavy glee,
While quartz sparkled, oh can't you see?
The rhythm was set by a sly little ant,
Who played the trumpet with a gallant chant!

The dirt clods cheered from the ground,
Creating echoes that bounced around.
Amidst the laughter, the symphony grew,
A harmony of earth in funny hues.

As the sun dipped low, the stones retired,
With tales of humor that never tired.
A melody of laughter, bright and bold,
In the symphony of stones, stories unfold!

www.ingramcontent.com/pod-product-compliance
Lightning Source LLC
Chambersburg PA
CBHW070307120526
44590CB00017B/2587